TRACEE L. PADILLA

Unveiled Again

*Ten Steps to Stop Losing Yourself and Start Living the
Life God Planted In You*

UNVEILED
Press *Living*

Contents

Introduction

If you and I were sitting together — probably with a cup of coffee, probably with me talking with my hands — and you asked, "Tracee, why did you write this book?" I wouldn't give you a perfect answer. I'd probably sigh, laugh at myself a little, and say something like:

"Because I know what it feels like to disappear inside your own life... and I know what it feels like to fight your way back."

I didn't lose myself all at once. It happened slowly. A little here, a little there. Kids. Ministry. Good seasons. Hard seasons. Divorce that shook everything I thought I knew about my future. The pressure to hold everything together. The weight of expectations — spoken and unspoken. Somewhere along the way, through all of it — the beautiful, the broken, and everything between — life formed this steady tide that pushed my own God-given dreams farther and farther into the background.

Life became whatever each day brought me instead of what I was deciding to bring to it.

And after a while, sitting in my office doing work that paid the bills but left my heart tired, I found myself staring at the wall wondering, "Is this really all there is?" I knew there was more in me. But after stepping away from ministry after divorce and landing in the corporate adminstrator world, it felt like every dream, calling, and God-whispered purpose had been placed on a library shelf somewhere... gathering dust.

If I'm being completely honest, I didn't know where to restart. Maybe you've felt that too.

You carry gifts and dreams that used to light you up — the kind that made you excited to wake up in the morning. You remember the visions God spoke into your heart, the ones that made you come alive. But somewhere along the way, life got loud. Other people's needs got louder. And the things God planted inside you? They went quiet. Smaller. Pushed into some "later" that never seems to come.

This book is the journey back.

Back to the version of you God always intended.

Not a "new you."

Not a "better you."

Just the real you — the one that got buried under years of doing, serving, surviving, pleasing, and holding everything together.

What I've learned — sometimes the hard way — is that you cannot step into the purpose God has for you while dragging around an identity He never asked you to wear. You can't walk confidently into your calling while feeling every fracture your past gave you. And you absolutely cannot build holy habits on a soul that's exhausted, unsure, or convinced it's unworthy.

This book is the heart work.

The soul work.

The "take a deep breath and remember who you are" work.

Before I started working on *Prothesis*, the message God gave me about purpose, pursuit, and intentional living, I've kept running into the same truth: people cannot build a life they don't believe they deserve. They can't step into purpose while shame is still whispering. They can't grow roots while their identity is unstable. And they can't form holy habits while their soul is running on empty.

So before I hand you rhythms, habits, structure, and a plan...

I needed to hand you **permission to breathe**.

That's what this book is.

It's the clearing of the soil before the seeds go in.

It's the gentle nudge that leans in and whispers, "Hey... you're still in there. Let's uncover what got buried."

Prothesis will guide you into purpose.

Holy Habits will help you live it out daily.

But this book?

This one is the coming home.

The remembering.

The uncovering.

The rising.

The letting go of layers that were never meant to define you in the first place.

So as you open these pages — a true prequel to *Prothesis: God's Purpose, My Pursuit* releasing early 2026 — I want to take you through something personal. Over the past 13 years, God has walked me through ten very real, very defining lessons. These are the truths that helped me take my own calling off the shelf where it had been collecting dust and learn how to walk forward again into the purpose He has for my life.

My prayer is that these same ten truths help you rise too — not by striving, not by hustling, but by remembering who you've always been in Him.

Let's begin.

> *Do not be afraid for I have ransomed you. I have called you by name; you are Mine. Isaiah 43:1*

1

The Discipline You Didn't Know You Needed

And the Lie That Kept You From Becoming Who You Were Created to Be

* * *

When I was younger, I had dreams — real, spark-in-your-eyes, this-is-what-I-was-born-for dreams. I wanted to write songs, travel and sing. Record albums and sit behind a piano and pour out my heart. And deep down, I wanted to write.

Stories. Books. Devotionals. All of it.

And I tried. Believe me, I tried. I blogged for a while. I wrote songs. I saved money for a demo reel. I bought CDs to sell at events. I had notebooks full of lyrics, half-finished chapters, outlines of dreams that kept me awake at night.

But if I'm being honest? Everything always seemed to fall flat. Not because I wasn't gifted. Not because God wasn't with me. Not because I lacked passion or calling. But because I lacked something I didn't even understand the value of yet:

Discipline.

Oof.

There it is.

The word nobody wants but everybody needs.

See, you don't have to be an early bird to fulfill your calling. But I was the girl staying up late, dragging myself out of bed in the morning like someone had chained concrete blocks to my ankles. I didn't understand that dreams don't grow because you feel them deeply — they grow because you show up consistently.

I didn't understand that writing requires rhythm. Blogging requires a schedule. Creativity needs structure. Purpose requires habits. Calling requires consistency.

I had discipline in chunks. My house was clean. The kids were fed. I could run a ministry. I could lead worship. I could tackle a to-do list like a CEO. But laundry? Don't ask. More about that in another chapter.

But the internal structure — the kind that organizes your life and aligns your daily choices with your vision and future self — that part was missing.

Not because I was lazy. Not because I wasn't capable. But because I was a **flow girl.** A wild-hearted, let's-see-where-today-goes girl. If I was surrounded by too much structure, I felt suffocated. But what I didn't realize, it was in the daily structure where true freedom would be found to begin to walk on the path of seeing God's purpose come alive in my life.

But here's what I didn't know just yet:

> *Even the most free-spirited person needs scaffolding if they want to build something that lasts.*

And then...

there's the lie.

The lie that sounds spiritual but kills more callings than anything I've ever seen.

You know the one.

"If God wants it to happen, He'll make it happen."

No.

Absolutely not.

Stop saying that.

Seriously.

I'm almost positive I said it at some point — and you may have too - maybe it was whispered on a tired day when nothing in your life felt like it was moving. But now? When I hear a someone say it, I want to lovingly grab them by the hand and say:

"That's not faith — that's a cop-out."

Because here's the truth:

The very dreams stirring in your heart...

that longing to write a book...

that passion to help single moms...

that tug to start a ministry...

those ideas you've carried for YEARS...

They're not going to start themselves.

Is there God timing?

Absolutely. But God timing isn't an excuse to not do anything at all. It's not permission to sit on what He planted. And it's definitely not a pass to ignore the daily habits that prepare you for what's coming.

Imagine God placing a beautifully wrapped gift right in front of you — not across the room, not hidden in a closet, not locked behind twelve secret doors — but literally right in front of you.

It has your name on it.

It's yours.

It's already been paid for.

But here's the part we don't like to admit:

God won't open the gift for you.

He won't rip the paper.

He won't lift the lid.

You have to reach out and take hold of it.

Many of us sit and stare at the box and say,

"Well... if God wants me to have it, He'll hand it to me."

No.

He already DID.

Now He's waiting on you to unwrap what He has already made available.

God gives the promise —

but you unwrap it.

God opens the door —

but you walk through it.

God calls —

but you respond.

The greatest revelation I've learned since those younger years is this:

Unwrapping the gift happens one small act at a time.

Not in giant leaps.

Not in overnight breakthroughs.

In the tiny, ordinary, almost invisible choices you make every day.

> *You have to start small.*
> *And you have to start now.*

Wake up early — even if it's just 20 minutes before the house comes alive.

Make your bed — not because it's pretty, but because discipline grows in the cracks.

Open your Bible — not at random, but daily.

Show up to your everyday life with intention and small acts of faithfulness.

Because here's what I've learned along the way:

Small faithfulness becomes holy momentum.

Small habits become holy habits.

Small beginnings become destiny-shifting movement.

And when it's time — truly God's time — for you to step into your calling?

You won't just be gifted.

You'll be ready.

Small Beginnings Matter

Here's the part most people miss about stepping into what God has called you to do, and trust me, I was one of them:

The supernatural is usually unlocked through the smallest natural steps.

He's not asking you to leap into the deep end. He's asking you to take the first step onto the shore.

And that's why this verse makes me smile every time I read it:

> "Do not despise these small beginnings, for the Lord rejoices to see the work begin..."
> Zechariah 4:10

We spend so much of our lives looking for the big break, the spotlight moment, the obvious "God is moving!" miracle — but

Scripture tells us the Lord gets excited long before that.

He doesn't just celebrate the finish line.

He celebrates the first step.

That word *rejoices* in Hebrew — *sameach* — means *to delight in, to be glad, to celebrate with joy.*

It's the picture of a Father watching His child toddle forward for the very first time... wobbly, unsteady, unsure, but *moving.*

And that image gets me every single time.

It reminds me of when my kids were little.

Their first steps.

Their first words.

The way their eyes lit up at the zoo, or when they did something brave, or when life surprised them with something brand new.

I used to think,

"I love seeing life through their precious little eyes..." And that hasn't changed even in their adult years as they're discovering the treasures God has for them. Seeing their dreams come alive and the prophetic things the Lord spoke to me about them and watching it come into fruition.

And I believe with my whole heart that the Lord looks at *us* the same way.

The first time you took a job that stretched your faith.

The first time you held your baby and felt overwhelmed by love and responsibility.

The first time you stepped into something terrifying but obeyed Him anyway.

He watched you with joy — not because you nailed it, but because you *began.*

And when you begin means you're choosing to trust Him because He already knows what's ahead. He knows the beauty hidden in the journey you haven't seen yet. He knows every treasure that will be uncovered step by step. And just like a good Father, He delights in watching you discover it.

So let this sink in:

Your Heavenly Father celebrates the moment you choose to...

· set your alarm 30 minutes early just to be with Him
· open your Bible when no one else sees
· write one paragraph in a journal you've ignored for years
· take one walk toward better health
· commit to a habit you've put off for a decade
· try again after you've failed 29 times

· show up — even when your confidence feels paper-thin

He rejoices to see the work begin...

even if no one else notices yet.
Heaven notices your small.
Heaven honors your tiny.
Heaven celebrates your first step —
just as loudly as your finish line.

If there's anything I want you to take from this chapter, it's this: you're not behind, you're not disqualified, and you're not too late. You are simply standing at the starting line of something God has been preparing you for all along and He knew the delays that would come along the way as well. Don't wait for the perfect moment any longer. Don't wait for the applause. Don't wait to feel "ready." Start small. Start now. Start with God. Every tiny yes is unwrapping the life He always meant for you to live no matter what age you are.

* * *

What I Learned — Chapter 1

The Discipline You Didn't Know You Needed

I learned that dreams don't grow on desire alone — they grow on discipline. The life God planted in me needed steady rhythms long before it needed big moments. Small obedience is never small to God, and showing up daily became the seed that changed everything.

* * *

Think About It

1. What "small beginning" is God asking me to stop overlooking and finally honor?
2. Where have I believed God only moves through big, obvious moments?
3. What tiny, faithful step can I begin this week?
4. In what area of my life do I sense God delighting in my beginning?

Prayer

Father, thank You for rejoicing over my small beginnings. Teach me not to despise the tiny steps or rush the process. Give me grace to begin, even when I feel behind. Help me show up with faithfulness, knowing You are celebrating every step I take toward the life You planted in me. Amen.

2

Quit Shrinking Your God-Given Gifting

Permission to Be Who God Called You to Be

* * *

Have you ever felt like you needed permission to be who God already called you to be?

Like you were waiting for someone — a pastor, a leader, a spouse, a friend, a parent — to tap you on the shoulder and whisper:

"Okay, now you can step into your gifting."

But here's the truth that might shake you a little:

Heaven never asked anyone else to authorize what God already appointed.

You don't need a committee.

You don't need someone to notice you first.

If God said it, heaven already stamped it.

IMPORTANT CLARIFICATION (So We Don't Misunderstand Each Other)

Now, before I go any further, let me say this with all the love in my heart because I am *not* talking about an "I don't need authority, I'll do what I want" spirit.

Absolutely not.

There *are* places in life — especially inside the church — where you absolutely need pastoral blessing, oversight, and permission.

- Starting a ministry.
- Launching a group.
- Stepping into certain leadership roles.
- Serving in positions that influence the body.

A healthy covering provides protection, accountability, stewardship, and wisdom — and God uses it to shape you.

Calling does not cancel covering and obedience is never rebellion.

So when I say you don't need permission, I'm talking about **identity**, not **assignment structure**.

You don't need a pastor to tell you you're called — God already said you are.

But yes, you may need their leadership to help guide how that calling is lived out.

So let's be clear:

You don't need permission to BE who God created you to be...

but you DO need covering as you WALK IT OUT.

Your shine should always live in the safety of godly alignment, not independence.

Okay — now with that foundation laid, let's go back to David.

Let me take you to a story in Scripture that inspires me every time I read it.

Remember David? The kid with the slingshot.

When Samuel came to Jesse's house to anoint the next king of Israel, nobody — and I mean nobody — even thought to bring David inside. His own father left him out in the field.

Everyone else lined up:

the strong ones,

the tall ones,

the impressive ones,

the ones who looked the part.

But David?

The one God had chosen?

He was overlooked.

Dismissed.

Not even invited to the room.

And here's the part that gets me:

David didn't shrink back because others didn't see him. He didn't let their assumptions define his identity. He didn't spend his life waiting for someone to validate his calling.

David knew who he was because he knew Whose he was.

And while everyone else was busy performing, posturing, or trying to look qualified, David was out in the field — tending sheep, writing songs, worshipping God, fighting lions and bears, growing into the calling God had placed on his life long before anyone else noticed.

God saw him long before man approved him.

And when the moment came?

Samuel didn't ask Jesse for permission.

He didn't check the family ranking.

He didn't follow the tradition.

He said,

"Send for him; we will not sit down until he comes." (1 Samuel 16:11)

In other words:

"We are not moving forward until the one God chose steps into the room."

Do you hear that?

God didn't wait for David to be validated by people.

God validated him Himself.

Hiding Behind the Lens of Insecurity

And here's where this hits close to home...

One thing you may not know about me is that growing up — and honestly, well into my adult years — I hid behind the lens of insecurity.

Yes, I said it.

And if you know me now you might be thinking,

"You? Insecure? No way!"

I get it. I lead worship every Sunday. I step out prophetically when the Holy Spirit nudges me. I speak, I teach, I do Bible studies, I write, I lead, I pour out.

But here's what you don't see: Every one of those moments requires me to cling — with white knuckles sometimes — to the hands of my Father. Because I cannot do anything God has called me to do without Him.

If Tracee had to do all that on her own? She would fall apart in two seconds flat.

I would stare out into a room full of people looking back at me and feel the urge to run.

I would doubt every word coming out of my mouth.

I would shrink into the smallest version of myself just to survive the moment.

I've had times where I was about to teach a Bible study and had to hide behind the whiteboard because I was having a full-on anxiety attack.

I've stood backstage during worship, heart racing, hands shaking, whispering,

"Lord, I can't do this unless You breathe through me."

And yet...

That same little girl — the one who spent years fighting insecurity — has also been determined.

Determined that insecurity does not get the final say.

Determined that insecurity does not get to silence the Spirit.

Determined that insecurity does not get to choose the story.

So when the Holy Spirit whispers:

"Speak this word..."

"Play this song..."

"Lead this moment..."

"Teach this study..."

"Start this podcast..."

"Write this book..."

I may be shaking, but I obey.

Because insecurity is loud —

but the Holy Spirit is louder.

And His voice wins.

You Are the Light of the World

Let's take a deeper dive into a conversation Jesus had with His disciples that will help us gain a greater revelation of the life we are to life. And what I love is, Jesus didn't tiptoe around identity when He spoke to them. He didn't say it softly or with hesitation. He declared it straight out and it's something we truly need to understand:

> "You are the light of the world — like a city on a hilltop that cannot be hidden.
>   No one lights a lamp and then puts it under a basket…"
>   Matthew 5:14–15

When Jesus said this, **"You are the light of the world,"** He wasn't telling His disciples to *try harder* to be good Christians. He was making a **declaration of identity** (that's fire!) rooted in who they belonged to and what they carried *because* of Him.

In Scripture, *light* always represents:

· **truth**
· **revelation**
· **purity**
· **God's presence**
· **the way forward**
· **the character of God Himself**

So when Jesus called His followers "the light," He was saying:
"Because My Spirit is in you, you now carry My presence, My truth, and My life into a world that is spiritually dark."

It's not about personality.

It's not about gifting.

It's not about confidence or boldness or extroversion.

It's about **reflection**.

We don't create the light.

We reflect the One who IS the light.

Just like the moon has no light of its own but shines because it reflects the sun, you shine because you reflect the Son. And get this, your God-given purpose and calling has everything to do with reflecting His light.

Why A City on a Hill?

Jesus didn't say:

"You're a candle hiding in the corner."

"You're a spark struggling to survive."

"You're a light trying your best."

He said:

"You are a city on a hill."

In Israel, back in the day, cities were built on hills for **visibility and safety**.

At night, their lamps could be seen for miles.

It was like Jesus was saying:

"You are meant to be seen. Your life is meant to point the way. Your faith is meant to be visible and unashamed."

Not because of ego, but, because **your visibility through what God has designed you to do and live leads others to God.** It's like this beautiful circle which is what my upcoming book, Prothesis: God's Plan, My Pursuit - is going to take a deeper dive into.

No One Lights a Lamp to Hide It

This part is SO important:

When Jesus says,

"No one lights a lamp and puts it under a basket,"

He's revealing God's heart:

God doesn't ignite you to hide you.

He doesn't anoint you to silence you.

He doesn't call you to conceal you.

He doesn't gift you to tuck you in the corner.

If God lights a lamp, He intends for that lamp to **shine**.

Covering your light doesn't make you humble.

It makes your God look smaller than He is.

And my friend, God is not small so it's time we stop living a life of small faith.

The Purpose of Your Light

Jesus ends the passage with this:

"...so that they may see your good works and glorify your Father in heaven."

Meaning:

Your light isn't about attention.

It's about **direction**.

Your life—your obedience, your story, your gifting, your glow—exists to point people to **Him**.

Light reveals the way.

Light exposes hope.

Light brings clarity.

Light pushes back darkness.

Light shows what's true.

Light makes it possible to move forward.

That's what your life does in the world.

You're not meant to blend in.

You're meant to illuminate the light of Jesus everywhere you go.

"You are the light of the world" means that through Jesus, you carry God's presence, truth, and hope into dark places — and your life was designed to shine openly, boldly, and beautifully so others can see Him through you.

It's Time to Throw Away the Basket

I want to remind you that the enemy wants you to keep your light hidden in a basket. And if you're wondering what that looks like, here are a few examples:

Insecurity is a basket.

Fear is a basket.

Comparison is a basket.

Imposter syndrome is a basket.

Waiting for approval is a basket.

Shrinking yourself is a basket.

Speaking doubt is a basket.

Not doing anything at all is a basket.

But here's what all of this comes down to:

God never hides what He lights.

If God put a fire in you —

a gift, a voice, a calling, a story, a song, a dream, a vision, an anointing —

He fully intends for it to SHINE.

He doesn't dim what He designed.

He doesn't mute what He anoints.

He doesn't shrink what He plans to use.

Just like He left David outside the room long enough for the truth to be obvious:

> *Man overlooks, but God appoints.*
>   *Man forgets, but God remembers.*
>   *Man sees the outside, but God sees the calling.*

And when *He* lights you, your shining is a reflection of His image through your life —
   it's obedience.
   It's stewardship.
   It's alignment.
   Your light points back to Him.

> *God never once asked you to shrink to fit a room He called you to stand in.*

He never asked you to quiet a voice He Himself breathed into existence.
   He never asked you to wait for confidence or validation to walk in what He already placed inside you.
   David wasn't chosen because he was impressive. He was chosen because he was His. And the same goes for you.
   Let me remind you again:
   Your insecurity doesn't disqualify you.
   Your past doesn't disqualify you.
   Your failures don't disqualify you.
   Your starting point doesn't disqualify you.

> *You are not fighting for identity — you're living FROM*

it.

That's why your obedience matters.

That's why courage matters.

That's why showing up — shaky hands and all — matters.

Because every time you obey the whisper of the Holy Spirit...

every time you step out when insecurity says "stay small"...

every time you trust God more than the noise around you or the fear inside you...

you are becoming the person God already sees.

So hear me when I say this with all the authority of a woman who has lived it:

Stop shrinking your God-given gift.

Stop waiting for someone else to give you permission.

Stop apologizing for the fire God put in your bones.

Walk boldly.

Walk faithfully.

Walk covered.

Walk obedient.

Walk lit by the One who called you long before anyone else had an opinion.

Because the world doesn't need a smaller version of who God made you to be.

It needs a person who knows they were chosen —

and lives like it.

* * *

What I Learned — Chapter 2

Permission to Be Who God Called You to Be

I learned that I don't need the world's permission to be who God says I already am. Insecurity may whisper loud, but identity in Christ always speaks louder. God didn't call me to hide — He called me to stand in who He created me to be.

* * *

Think About It

1. Where am I hiding the light God placed in me out of insecurity or fear?
2. What gifting or calling have I been treating like it needs someone else's permission?
3. If I stopped shrinking and started shining, what would I dare to step into?
4. What "basket" have I placed over my light that God is calling me to remove?

Prayer

Lord, thank You for calling me light — even in the places where I've felt small, unsure, or insecure. Forgive me for hiding what You have placed inside me. Give me courage to step out, speak up, and shine with boldness and humility. Let every gift You've placed in me bring glory to You, not me. Help me silence insecurity and follow the whisper of Your Spirit above every other voice. Teach me to shine without apology—just as You created me to. Amen.

3

Love Isn't Earned by Overdoing

You Were Loved Before You Ever Lifted a Finger

* * *

We've all been there. Especially if we're moms, dads, wives, husbands, leaders, caretakers, the "responsible one," the "strong one," or the "Hey, can you help me real quick?" one. That quiet ache slips in without warning—the belief that if we do just a little more, give a little more, serve a little harder, or keep everything running smoothly, maybe we'll finally feel enough. Maybe we'll feel valuable or appreciated or worthy. Maybe if we keep the house spotless, say yes to everything, anticipate every need, or never drop the ball, then the inside of us will finally feel steady too.

And here's where the trap gets sneaky:

Some of the pressure comes from *people* — wanting to keep everyone happy.

And some of the pressure comes from *our misunderstanding of*

God — feeling like we need to work to keep Him pleased.

Those two things look different on the outside, but they drain you the same way on the inside. Because whether you're trying to earn someone's approval or trying to earn God's love, you end up carrying a weight you were never designed to hold.

But the truth that sets you free is this: you were loved long before you ever lifted a finger. Before you cooked the meal, folded the laundry, said yes when you were exhausted, or carried someone else's load, God had already called you His. He had already delighted in you. He had already named you His heir.

You don't serve FOR love — you serve FROM love.

And that changes everything.

The problem is, sometimes the hustle doesn't come out of the genuine love to serve, but being afraid of disappointing people. We're afraid stillness will look like laziness. We worry rest will be misunderstood as weakness. We think boundaries mean we're selfish (we'll talk more about that in chapter 4). And slowing down? That feels like spiritual failure.

Ministry makes this even more complicated. It's easy to assume that the busier we are for God, the more spiritual we must be. We start believing that showing up early, staying late, filling every gap, and saying yes to every need is proof of our devotion. Without realizing it, we carry our overloaded schedules almost like trophies. That quiet voice whispers, "Look at me, Lord—I'm doing this for You," as if God is somehow impressed with our exhaustion.

But in reality, never once did the Lord ever ask us to live this way.

If you haven't noticed, overdoing never delivers what it

promises.

Being needed isn't the same as being valued.

Being busy doesn't equal being connected.

And being productive cannot substitute being loved.

When serving is fueled by people-pleasing, guilt, or insecurity — or simply believing "this is the Christian thing to do" — this is where your soul begins to crack. The constant motion of constantly doing drowns out the very voice we're trying to follow. It becomes more distraction than devotion. And the saddest part? We don't even recognize how heavy the load has become because we've carried it so long, we just call it normal.

Think of it this way: God never asked you to become His employee. He asked you to be His beloved. He didn't create you to hustle so that you'd receive His approval. He created you to live from His love — *a love that you never have to earn.* Thank you, Father!

And that's exactly why the story of Martha and Mary speaks volumes... Every time I read it (Luke 10:38-42), something in me stops. Why? Because I can be a Martha more times that I'd like to admit and I need this continual reminder.

Mary Has Chosen the Better Part

The scene is simple:

Jesus walks into their home.

Mary sits at His feet — still, present, unhurried, unashamed.

Eager to learn, grow, and take the moment in.

Martha, on the other hand?

She's in the kitchen,

hands full,

mind racing,

heart anxious,
as she pulls out her Joanna Gaines latest cookbook,
trying to figure out what to make for dinner (totally paraphrasing here...)
trying to be the hostess with the mostest,
trying to serve well
trying to look like she has it all together,
trying to do everything right. Phew!
Sound familiar?
And the words that come out of her mouth?
"Lord, don't You care...?"
that is the heartbeat of an over-functioning believer.
It's frustration.
It's striving.
It's exhaustion.
It's insecurity wrapped in responsibility.
"Don't You care that I'm carrying all of this?
Don't You see everything I'm doing?
Don't You notice how hard I'm working?
Don't You see me being the responsible one?
Doesn't any of this matter?"
And Jesus — full of compassion — doesn't rebuke her effort. He doesn't shame her serving. He doesn't tell her she's wrong. He speaks to her *heart*:

> "Martha, Martha...you are worried and upset over all these details.
> But only one thing is necessary. Mary has chosen the better part..."
> Luke 10:41–42

Do you know what He was really saying?

"You're serving like an employee.
But I invited you as a daughter."

He wasn't asking Martha to stop serving —but what He doing was inviting her to stop striving. He wasn't calling her out —He was calling her *in. In to the intimate places with Him.*

He wanted her heart before her work.

Presence *before* the constant pressure of doing.

Connection *before* contribution.

You see, serving isn't wrong.

But serving from worry?

Serving from exhaustion?

Serving from insecurity?

Serving from "maybe this will make me feel good enough"?

Serving from "if I just do more "?

Serving from "this is Christian thing to do"?

Serving from "I'll be accepted"?

Serving from "being busy means I'm spiritual"?

Serving from "trying to earn God's love"?

That's where we lose our focus of what it's truly all about.

Once again, Martha wasn't wrong for working hard. She was wrong for thinking that hard work was the thing that was right to do in that moment. More important than sitting at the feet of Jesus.

And can I just say...

don't we do the same?

I know I surely have.

We say things, like:

· "If I don't do it, then who will?"
· "This is what servant leadership looks like."

· "If I keep giving, God will reward me."
· "What I do for God defines how much God loves me."
· "If I volunteer more I'll feel validated."

And Jesus whispers the same words He whispered then:
"Come sit.
Come rest.
Come be with Me.
You don't have to earn what I freely give."

Where Healing Truly Begins

While there is something absolutely beautiful about giving to others and having a servant's heart—truly nothing like it—and yes, it's vitally important, it will never be what enables us to earn the love of God. Why? Because He already gave us His love. It was never about what we do, but who HE is. But here's the trap so many of us fall into: we start serving from fear instead of love, from pressure instead of presence, from the belief that if we just hold everything together a little tighter, maybe we'll finally feel worthy or spiritual or "enough." And maybe you've never considered this reality—that the very thing God has been whispering to you, the same thing He's whispered to me, isn't to stop caring or stop serving or lose the beautiful, nurturing, steady parts of who you are... but to stop believing that your worth hangs on how perfectly you perform.

He isn't asking you to abandon your strengths; He's asking you to stop confusing your strength with your identity. You don't have to live at the mercy of other people's expectations, and you don't have to earn the love that's already yours. This is where the paradigm shift of freedom begins—when you realize

God is not waiting for your effort, He's waiting for your heart.

Because the truth is, God never once asked us to live so busy, so frantic, so constantly "on" that we forget who He even is. That's why we end up running on fumes. That's why our faith feels thin and our peace keeps slipping through our fingers. We're pouring out without ever stopping to be poured into. We're calling our pace "godly" when it's actually the very thing the enemy hopes we'll keep doing. If he can keep us busy enough, hurried enough, responsible enough, distracted enough, then we won't slow down long enough to sit in the presence that actually restores us.

But something holy happens when you finally breathe, slow down, and let Him remind you who you are apart from all the doing. Something inside you settles. Your soul unclenches. Your identity anchors. You begin to move from striving to belonging... from proving to becoming... from working for love to living from it. And that—right there—is where healing truly begins.

* * *

What I Learned — Chapter 3

You Were Loved Before You Ever Lifted a Finger

I learned that God never asked me to outrun my exhaustion to prove my devotion. His love isn't earned by how well I serve, how much I carry, or how perfectly I hold everything together. He wants my heart more than my hustle. When I slow down long enough to sit at His feet instead of striving to impress Him—or anyone else—I remember the truth: I was loved before I ever lifted a finger, and nothing I do will ever make me more His than

I already am.

* * *

THINK ABOUT IT

1. Where have I been acting like God's employee instead of His daughter?
2. What part of my life feels overburdened because I'm over-performing instead of receiving love?
3. What do I fear will happen if I slow down or say no?
4. How is God inviting me to choose presence over performance right now?

Prayer

Lord, You know how easily I slip into overdoing — not because I want applause, but because somewhere inside I fear not being enough. Teach me to rest like Mary instead of striving like Martha. Remind me that I am loved because I'm Yours, not because I'm useful. Show me where I've turned serving into striving. Help me to sit at Your feet without guilt, shame, or pressure. Restore my heart with the truth that I am Your daughter — fully loved, fully seen, and fully held. Amen.

4

Letting Go of What Everyone Else Thinks

Learning to Set Holy Boundaries Without Guilt or Apology

* * *

We don't talk about this enough in the Church world...but "being available" is not the same as being obedient. And "being nice" is not the same as being healthy. There comes a point in your life — and it usually happens somewhere between revelation and breakthrough — where you realize:

> **If I don't learn how to set holy boundaries,**
> **I will keep living at the mercy of everyone else's expectations.**

If you haven't figured out by now, everyone has an idea of what you should do, how quickly you should respond, what you should carry, what you should fix, what you should take on, and who you should be for them. And if you're not careful, you'll spend your entire life running from one expectation to the next...never getting around to building the very thing God entrusted to you.

I remember once the company I worked for hired a new Vice President. He just so happened to be in a bluegrass band, so naturally one of the other VPs let him know that I played piano and sing. He got so excited and immediately said, "Hey, the next time we perform, you can play and sing with us." Not once did he ask if I'd be interested—he just assumed I'd want to join. A few weeks later, he brought me the dates of their performances and basically told me I'd be playing. I kindly let him know I wasn't interested. Honestly, he didn't take it well but I was totally OK with that. Just because he wanted me to, didn't mean that it was what I was supposed to do. That moment was the perfect example of this truth:

> **If I don't learn how to set boundaries, I will keep living at the mercy of everyone else's expectations.**

Knowing How to Say No

Let me take you to a story in Scripture that gives us the backbone we need to help us.

In the book of Nehemiah, God calls him to rebuild the broken walls of Jerusalem. It's a massive assignment.

Holy.

Strategic.

Important.

And not everyone is happy about it. (Shocking, I know)

People try to distract him. (Cue drama music)

Discourage him. (Ah, the gift of negativity)

Pull him away. (Because apparently no one else is available)

Make him question himself. (Gaslighting 101)
Demand his attention. (Um, please take a number)
Demand his time. (Hello, we're more important over here)
Demand his presence. (At this point I need a nap)
Sound familiar?

But Nehemiah had something many of us have struggled to learn:

He knew how to say no.

When four different messengers came to pull him off the wall —to interrupt him, to drag him into someone else's agenda, to get him involved in drama he didn't belong in —(hello, social media...lol!) Nehemiah didn't cave. He didn't apologize. He didn't over-explain. He didn't crumble under pressure. Instead he said one of the most powerful boundary lines in the Bible:

> "I am doing a great work and I cannot come down."
> Nehemiah 6:3

Read that again.

"I cannot come down."

Not because he didn't care. Not because he wasn't compassionate. Not because he didn't want peace. Not because he was being rude. But because he knew something we tend to forget:

> ***When you're building what God told you to build,***
> ***you don't come down for every cry, crisis, or opinion.***

So what do we do:
Stay focused.

Stay obedient.

Stay in alignment.

Stay exactly where God put you.

Because here's the thing: **if you answer every single "come down" moment?**

You won't be led by the Spirit — you'll be led by interruptions.

What looks like an opportunity can actually be a distraction.

What sounds urgent may not be important.

And what feels like an obligation may not be your assignment at all.

Nehemiah wasn't being rude — he was being faithful.

He wasn't pulling away — he was *staying in position.*

He wasn't dodging responsibility — he was *protecting his calling.*

There's a **big difference** between being *needed* and being *called.*

There's a **big difference** between being *available* and being *obedient.*

And there is a **massive difference** between being *godly* and being *drained.*

And in this season of your life, you need to learn this sentence too — not just in your mind, but deep in your bones:

"I'm doing a great work... and I cannot come down."

Because if the enemy can't stop you, he'll distract you.

And those distractions?

Oh, they don't show up wearing a neon sign that says "danger."

They show up looking like expectations, needs, "urgent" requests, or "just this one thing" moments.

Let me tell you something the younger Tracee had *no clue* about:

I didn't understand boundaries.

I didn't even know what they were.

The early version of me said yes because I didn't know I was *allowed* to say no.

I felt guilty for saying no.

It was the eager-to-please, hope-I'm-not-letting-anyone-down version of me.

And here's what happens when you don't know boundaries:

People don't just notice your gifting...

they start organizing their world around it.

Not maliciously.

Not manipulatively.

Just human nature.

People see:

- your leadership
- your excellence
- your faithfulness
- your creativity
- your voice
- your abilities
- your organizational ability
- your compassion
- your willingness

...and suddenly *your yes* becomes the easiest solution to someone else's assignment. Not because they're using you or don't care about you. But because your "yes" makes their life easier.

37

And don't get me wrong — there are seasons where God absolutely grows us through saying yes. There are opportunities that stretch us, shape us, build us, prune us, prepare us. But something shifted in me the last few years in a way I can't ignore:

Not everyone gets my yes anymore.

Even if it's something I love.
Even if it's something I'm good at.
Even if it looks like a "perfect fit."
Even if people say, "Oh this is SO you."
Even if it aligns with my gifting.
Because an invitation always has two answers:
yes or no.
And "no" is not a bad word.
I used to believe that if something was *possible*, it must automatically be *God's will for me.* If I could do it, I should do it mentality. But here's what I've learned — often the hard way:

Just because I can do it doesn't mean I'm called to it.

And some of the heaviest, most overwhelming seasons of my life came from **MY yes**, not God's assignment.
I put myself into them.
I overloaded myself.
I signed myself up for pressure God never handed me.
And I blamed the weight on "ministry" or "service," when the truth was — it was my lack of boundaries.
Now?
Now I'm learning to protect the yes God DID give me. To honor Him by staying attached to what HE assigned me to do - not

what people want to assign me to do. Because at the end of the day...I'm responsible for the calling He put on my life —not the ones people try to hand me along the way.

Boundaries Aren't Unkind — They're Biblical

Now let's talk about a part of boundaries related to God's Word that can get a little confusing at times to understand. It can be one of the biggest lies Christian women and men battle is this:

"If I set boundaries, I'm being selfish."

Let me lovingly tell you —

that's not Scripture.

And it's the reason so many of us:

· run ourselves into the ground,
· take on responsibilities God never assigned us,
· stay in unhealthy cycles,
· and confuse burnout with faithfulness.

The truth is:

Boundaries aren't walls.

They're clarity.

They're commitment.

They're stewardship.

They're obedience.

Dr. Henry Cloud — author of *Boundaries* — says something deeply true (paraphrased):

> *Boundaries don't make you selfish; they make you responsible for the life God gave you.*

39

Here's what we often misunderstand about boundaries:

they are not about **blocking people out**, they are about **keeping your God-given assignment in**. A boundary is simply the line that says, "This is mine to carry, and that is not." It defines where your responsibility ends and someone else's begins. Dr. Henry Cloud talks about this often (paraphrased): boundaries help you know what God made YOU the steward of — and what He did *not* make you the steward of. And when you blur those lines, you don't become more spiritual... you become more exhausted.

Biblical boundaries protect the soil of your life. They guard your emotional and spiritual capacity so you can actually obey what God has asked of you. Without boundaries, your heart gets pulled into every crisis, every expectation, every demand, every need — and before long, your "yes" becomes a reflex instead of a response to the Holy Spirit. That's when love turns into resentment. That's when serving turns into striving. That's when helping turns into overfunctioning.

Let me say this clearly:

Boundaries don't limit your love — they strengthen it.

They make your "yes" healthier, your "no" clearer, your obedience sharper, and your assignment protected. A life without boundaries doesn't make you more Christlike... it makes you more drained, distracted, and depleted.

Even Jesus Had Boundaries

And here is the most freeing revelation:

Even Jesus had boundaries.

Jesus.

The most compassionate, loving, servant-hearted person to

walk this earth...
He walked away from crowds.
He withdrew from people who needed Him.
He rested when others still wanted miracles.
He said no.
He disappeared for prayer.
He honored His assignment over everyone else's expectations.

Luke captures it perfectly:

> "But Jesus often withdrew to lonely places and prayed." Luke 5:16

Often.
Not rarely.
Not occasionally.
Not only in emergencies.
Often.

If Jesus didn't heal every person in every crowd,
why do we fall apart when we can't meet every expectation?

If Jesus said no to people,
why do we feel guilty doing the same?

If Jesus took time away to be restored,
why do we think rest is weakness?

If Jesus protected His assignment,
why do we think boundaries are selfish?

And let me give you another truth:

Some of the "good things" trying to pull you down from your wall aren't God things.

Nehemiah knew that.

Jesus knew that.

And now?

We need to learn this important life-changing lesson as well.

The beauty of this journey of living out God's purpose and plans for our life is learning to love from assignment, not expectation.

There is a difference — a holy, freeing difference — between:

being loving

and

being controlled by what people want from you

Between:

being helpful

and

being drained and resentful

Between:

being available

and

being obedient

And here's what I've discovered the hard way:

The more focused I become on what God assigned me to do, the fewer yes's I have available.

Not because I'm unwilling.

Not because I'm unloving.

But because following the Lord through obedience requires clarity - and clarity requires boundaries.

God didn't ask me to be Nehemiah AND Mary AND Martha AND the entire town of Jerusalem. He asked me to steward HIS calling He placed in me with excellence.

And sometimes that means saying:

- "I can't take that on right now."
- "That's not my assignment."
- "I'm honored you asked, but I have to say no."
- "I'm staying focused on what God is building in my life."
- "I'm doing a great work and cannot come down."

Boundaries don't push people away.

They keep you aligned.

They protect your yes.

They protect your peace.

They protect your purpose.

They protect your God-given capacity.

Remember as I say this on repeat:

If the enemy can't destroy you, he'll try to distract you.

Nehemiah knew it.

Jesus modeled it.

And *this* is where YOU begin to rise into it.

* * *

What I Learned — Chapter 4

Learning to Set Holy Boundaries Without Guilt or Apology

I learned that not everyone gets my yes — and that's not selfish, it's stewardship. God never asked me to be everything to everyone. He asked me to stay aligned with Him. Protecting my yes became a sacred act of obedience.

* * *

THINK ABOUT IT

1. Where am I saying yes out of guilt instead of obedience?
2. Who am I trying to keep happy at the expense of my peace and calling?
3. What "good things" are pulling me off the wall God assigned me to build?
4. What would protecting my yes look like in this next season?

Prayer

Lord, help me recognize the difference between what You've called me to do and what others are asking me to carry. Give me the courage to say no when I need to, the wisdom to guard the assignments You've entrusted to me, and the clarity to stay focused on what truly matters.

Teach me to be like Nehemiah — unshaken, undistracted, and faithful to the work You've placed before me. Help me honor my capacity, protect my peace, and remember that boundaries are not rebellion — they are obedience. Lead me into a life aligned with Your voice, not everyone else's expectations. Amen.

5

Stop Breaking Your Own Heart

Healing the Patterns That Pull You Back Into Old Cycles

* * *

Let me tell you something that I believe will truly set you free:

> *There comes a moment in every person's life where you have to stop blaming your past for the cycles you keep repeating... and finally tend to the wounds that keep pulling you backward.*

It's about the honest, brave realization that:

Sometimes the person hurting you the most... is the version of you that you haven't healed yet.

Read that again.

It took me a while to understand this. I thought the hidden frustrations I lived in was because of the heavy seasons I had walked in. Or what life demanded from me. Or because I was too

45

kind, too passionate, too sensitive, too willing, too "whatever."

But eventually, after walking through several trials, I began to see a common denominator that kept arising - leading me to take a look in the mirror and answer the harder question:

"Tracee, are you really growing in your walk, spiritually...or are their past wounds in your life you haven't healed from keeping you from growing forward?"

And the truth?

I realized I was the one that hadn't grown from past wounds or I was allowing others to reopen them.

And that right there — the not-growing, not-healing patterns — is where the real unraveling happens. You don't even see it at first. You're just trying to be a good wife, a good mom, a good Christian, a good *everything*. You're trying to keep peace. Hold it all together. Smile through things that should've broken you. And before you know it, the version of you showing up in your relationships isn't the strong one you *think* you are...it's the unhealed one silently running the show.

One of these areas I didn't see it in myself until someone said it out loud.

I'll never forget sitting across from my counselor during my divorce — a season that felt like someone had taken the floor out from under me. She listened. She nodded. And then she asked the question that made the room go quiet:

"Tracee... why do you allow yourself to become the carpet and let your husband walk all over you?"

My first reaction? Absolutely not. That's not me. I'm strong. I don't let people walk all over me. I love the Lord. I know who I am.

But the truth? The truth stung because it was real.

I *had* allowed myself to shrink. I had allowed fear to silence my own voice. I had tried so hard to keep the atmosphere joyful in my home for too many years that I slowly disappeared inside it. I wasn't being a peacemaker...I was being a peace-keeper, and peace-keeping always costs you pieces of yourself.

And God never—**never**—asked me to live like that.

That moment with my counselor became a turning point, because it forced me to face what so many of us don't want to admit:

Sometimes the pattern we keep blaming on other people...

is actually the part of *us* that hasn't healed yet.

And granted, sometimes healing can't take place until you've removed yourself from the toxic environment you've been living in.

The Painful Cycle Nobody Talks About

If you've ever found yourself doing any of these...

- staying in places you've outgrown
- saying yes when your spirit is screaming no
- tolerating treatment far beneath how God sees you
- excusing behavior you would never advise another person to accept
- shrinking yourself to keep the peace
- ignoring your God-given cues because "it's easier"
- sabotaging good opportunities because you're scared
- running back to what hurt you because it's familiar
- believing this is the best it'll ever be

...then let me gently tell you:

You're not crazy.

You're not weak.

47

You're not broken.

You're simply **living from an unhealed version of yourself.**

The version who learned to survive.

The version who learned to keep everyone else happy.

The version who learned to keep quiet.

The version who learned to stay small.

The version who learned to prove their worth.

The version who learned chaos as normal.

The version who learned "love means over-functioning."

The version who learned to work for belonging instead of receiving it.

And that version is exhausted.

But here's the beautiful news:

You don't have to keep abandoning yourself.

Healing isn't becoming someone else.

Healing is coming home to the person God actually created you to be.

Let's Talk About the Script You've Been Living Under

Everyone has a script that once helped them survive...

but eventually starts to feel suffocating.

Maybe yours sounds like:

· "I have to keep everyone happy."
· "I'm not enough."
· "I'll just mess it up."
· "I don't deserve better."
· "I should just be grateful for what I have."
· "Good things aren't for people like me."
· "If I don't fix it, no one will."
· "If I don't keep the peace, everything will fall apart."

· "If I rest, I'm being lazy."
· "Better stay small than risk being misunderstood."

But let me tell you, for years after my divorce —as a former pastor's wife, a worship leader, and someone who loved ministry with my whole heart —I felt like I had lost every part of who I was.

I remember one day opening my jewelry box and "grabbing" something that wasn't even there — an imaginary, obnoxiously large necklace with a **giant D on it.**

D for divorced.

D for damaged.

D for disqualified.

Now, nobody handed it to me. God certainly didn't place it on me. No angel from heaven came down and fastened it around my neck. But *I* wore it. And I carried it like it was the only identity I had left.

And the weight?

Oh, it was heavy.

That part of my story still breaks me a little if I'm honest. Not because of shame — God has healed that —but because of how much I let it define me.

I truly believed everyone saw me through that label. I believed God couldn't use me anymore. I believed my purpose had expired. I believed every dream had shattered —ministry, calling, writing, worship...all of it.

But God...He has a way of stepping right into the middle of our self-imposed labels.

I'll never forget sitting in a restaurant during a business lunch. I had just met a woman who was part of a prayer ministry — and she just so happen to be a powerhouse prayer warrior —

and without knowing **anything** about me, she suddenly looked straight into my eyes and said:

> *"You have been carrying a weight — a weight of shame.*
> *And the Lord says it's time to take it off.*
> *That is NOT who you are...*
> *and NOT how He sees you."*

And right there — in the middle of a restaurant —with people eating their sandwiches and minding their own business, she laid her hands on my head and prayed OUT LOUD. I didn't care who heard. Because I knew...it was time. Time to take off the necklace. Time to stop agreeing with lies God never authored. Time to walk forward into the future He still had planned. He had never place that necklace around my neck and that day, He took it off of me.

And let me tell you something important:

God's purpose for your life is not canceled by the chapters you didn't expect.

Just because divorce was in my story did NOT mean disqualified was my identity.

Did people judge?

Oh, yes.

Some people are gifted in the ministry of gossip instead of grace.

But you learn this:

You don't owe anyone a defense or an explanation.

You owe God your obedience.

They didn't walk through your fire.

They didn't walk in your shoes.

They didn't weep your tears.

They didn't fight your battles.

They didn't sit with you in your lonely nights.

They didn't hear your cries out to the Lord for help.

They didn't hear God whisper over you when you thought your life was over.

So don't waste your breath proving anything to them. Just keep walking forward —hand in hand with the Father —because His Word never disqualified you.

Because here's what I had to learn the hard way:

The same God who washed the shame off of me is the same God who has done this for every one of His children since the beginning of time. We tend to act like we're the exception — like somehow our mistakes, our story, our trauma, our past makes *us* the one person God might be hesitant to redeem. But the Bible tells a very different story.

Scripture is literally filled with men and women who had chapters they weren't proud of... chapters the world would've used to write them off. Yet God never flinched. He never hesitated. He never said, "Too far gone." Instead, He picked them up, breathed purpose into them, and wrote redemption so loudly through their lives that we're still talking about them today.

Moses the murderer.

David the adulterer.

Rahab the prostitute.

Peter the denier.

Jacob the deceiver.

Paul the persecutor.

You know... all the people God used to shape the very story of redemption.

If God disqualified people based on the worst chapter of their lives, the Bible would be one very short book.

But here's the truth that will set your heart free:

God builds His Kingdom through redemption.

I need to say that again.

God doesn't build His kingdom on a person's perfect story.

He builds it on the power of redemption!

He builds it on people who fall down, get up, and keep walking.

People who have scars but also have surrender.

People who have history but also have hunger.

People who thought they were done, but God whispered, "I'm not finished."

Your past doesn't get the right to define who you are today.

Your mistakes may mark a moment, but they do not mark your identity.

And your most painful chapter is often the birthplace of your greatest calling.

The very people others counted out...

God counted *in*.

On purpose.

With purpose.

For purpose.

So if the enemy has tried to convince you that your story disqualified you, let me lovingly remind you:

You are exactly the kind of person God writes destinies through.

Not because you're flawless,

but because you're willing.

Not because you've never failed,

but because you've learned who your Father is in the middle of your failures.

Not because your past is pretty,

but because His grace is powerful.

And if He can rebuild Moses, David, Rahab, Peter, Jacob, and Paul and countless others...

He can rebuild you too — beautifully, completely, and without hesitation.

It's Time to Come Home

Let me bring you into a story Jesus told about the prodigal son.

And maybe you're thinking, "Okay, Tracee... but I've never lived a wild prodigal life."

Fair. Many of us haven't. I've walked with the Lord since I was 9 years old, so I get it. But hear me — you don't have to wander into a distant country to feel far from God. Sometimes it's the battles we didn't choose... the heartbreaks we didn't see coming... the disappointments that bruised our identity... the chapters we didn't plan... that make us feel unworthy.

You can love Jesus with your whole heart and still feel marked by your past.

You can serve faithfully and still feel like you've somehow disqualified yourself.

You can be in church every week and still carry the quiet ache of "Maybe I messed up too much... maybe I'm too broken... maybe God is done with me."

But that's exactly why Jesus told the story He did.

It's the story of **redemption.**

When the prodigal son came home...

He was messy.

He was ashamed.

He was rehearsing his apology.

He had already demoted himself to "servant-level" in his

mind.

He believed he no longer deserved belonging.

And what did the Father do?

He ran.

He embraced him.

He covered him.

He restored him.

He called him "son" again before the boy ever performed a single good deed.

The Father didn't say:

- "Explain yourself."
- "Earn your place back."
- "Let's go over your mistakes."
- "I need you to work harder this time."

No.

He said:

"Bring the robe. Bring the ring. My son is home."

Why does this matter?

Because so many of us keep breaking our own hearts by punishing ourselves for things God has already forgiven. We act like servants in a house where we were meant to be sons and daughters. We downgrade ourselves because of past decisions, past seasons, past pain...when God is standing there with a robe, a ring, and a feast saying:

"Come home to who I created you to be.

No more starving yourself of grace. No more punishing yourself. No more living from the old scripts. No more labeling yourself with a label God never spoke over you. No more loosing your voice because you're were walking in fear.

This is where healing begins. You see,

God never asked me to wear a necklace with a D on it.

He always wanted to clothe me in restoration and He wants to do the same for you.

The prodigal didn't earn his way home.

He was welcomed home because he belonged.

And that is the truth that dismantles every old script you've ever lived under.

The Joy of the Lord is Your Strength

Before we close this chapter, I need to take you to one more moment in Scripture — and this just so happens to be my life verse. I can't think of a better way to bring this home.

Let me paint the backstory for you, because it matters.

God's people had just returned from Babylonian exile — **seventy long years** in a foreign land, decades of hardship, loss, confusion, and identity-shaking disappointment. When they finally returned to Jerusalem, the first thing they rebuilt wasn't the temple. It wasn't their homes. It wasn't their routines.

It was the wall.

Why?

Because the wall symbolized strength, safety, and identity.

A rebuilt wall meant:

"We're not ruined anymore. We're protected again. We belong here."

Under Nehemiah's leadership (the man who understood the importance of boundaries), the work was grueling, resisted, attacked, mocked, and opposed. But they stayed faithful, brick by brick, until finally — the wall was complete.

And then something beautiful happened.

The people gathered in the square, and Ezra opened the Book of the Law — Scripture many of them had **never heard in their lifetime.** The moment the Word was read, the people began to weep. Not quiet tears. **Chest-shaking sobs.** Tears of regret. Tears of recognition. Tears from a lifetime of feeling far from God.

They were feeling the weight of their past.

And Ezra could have said,

"You should feel this. You messed up."

He could have said,

"Now you must earn your way back."

But he didn't.

Instead, he said something that we need to carry with us:

"Do not grieve, for the joy of the Lord is your strength." — Nehemiah 8:10

In other words:

"This is not a day for shame.

This is a day for celebration."

"This isn't the moment to punish yourself.

This is the moment to remember who your God is."

"Your restoration is not a funeral.

It's a feast."

Ezra literally told them to go eat rich foods, drink sweet drinks, and celebrate — not because they were perfect, but because **God had brought them home.**

Do you see it?

Just like the prodigal son

Just like the robe and the ring

Just like the Father running to embrace His child

God's heart is not for you to stay stuck in grief over who you were.

His heart is for you to step into joy as He rebuilds who you are.

You don't heal by mourning your past forever.

You heal by letting God turn your mourning into dancing.

You heal by letting His joy steady your steps again.

You heal by tasting the goodness of a God who restores — completely.

The joy of the Lord isn't a feeling.

It's the strength that fills you when you finally come home.

So as you close this chapter — with all its honesty, all its confession, all its naming of old patterns — I want you to hear this with tenderness:

Do not grieve anymore.

Not over what God already redeemed.

Not over the chapters He already covered.

Not over the labels He never wrote.

Not over the lies He tore off.

Lift your head, child of God.

The wall is being rebuilt.

The Father has run to meet you.

The table is set.

And joy — real joy — is waiting for you to taste it.

Because **the joy of the Lord is your strength.**

This is where healing begins.

* * *

What I Learned — Chapter 5

Healing the Patterns That Pull You Back Into Old Cycles

I learned that shame loses its voice the moment I stop agreeing with it. The labels life tried to stick on me were never mine to wear — and every time I let God peel one off, I could breathe again. Healing wasn't about becoming a stronger version of the old me; it was about finally coming home to who He created me to be. And identity... true identity... is restored one surrendered piece at a time, because the joy of the Lord IS my strength.

* * *

THINK ABOUT IT

1. What patterns in my life keep repeating because I haven't healed the root?
2. Where am I still treating myself like a servant instead of a beloved daughter?
3. Which old lies am I still obeying... and what truth does God speak instead?
4. What would "coming home to myself" look like in this season?

Prayer

Lord, help me stop breaking my own heart with the old patterns I've carried for years. Heal the places I've ignored, the wounds I've learned to live with, and the lies I've believed about who I am. Teach me to receive Your love without earning it, Your grace without question, and Your identity over me without hesitation. Show me the places where old versions of me are still leading, and gently bring me back home to the daughter You created me to be. Restore me like the Father restored the prodigal — fully, joyfully, completely. Amen.

6

Show Up Anyway

How God Uses Ordinary, Imperfect, Still-Healing People to Do Extraordinary Things

* * *

I think most of us have grown up with this thinking that God only uses the people who have it all together — the confident ones, the put together ones, the ones who never miss a beat and can quote Scripture at lightning speed. You know, the ones you see on your Instagram Reel, right?

But here's the truth:

God rarely picks the person who looks like the obvious choice.

He looks for the person who is willing to show up, knees shaking and all.

And if there's one thing I've learned about walking with God, it's this:

I almost never felt qualified for the assignments He handed me.

But even in that uncertainty, I learned how to say yes anyway.

Moses — The Man Who Tried to Talk God Out of Using Him

One of the clearest examples of this is Moses. I love Moses because he is so relatable. When God showed up and called him, Moses didn't give some strong, bold "Here I am, send me" speech. Instead, he gave God a grocery list of reasons why he was the wrong guy. "Who am I?" "What if they won't listen?" "I'm not a good speaker." "My words get tangled." He even flat-out said, "Lord... please send someone else." If Moses had a LinkedIn profile, he would have deleted it right then and there.

Moses, the man we preach about, write about, admire, and quote, basically told God:

"I don't think You picked the right person."

But God didn't flinch. He didn't say, "You're right, Moses, what was I thinking! You are a terrible public speaker. Let me go find someone more put together." He didn't ask Moses to go work on his confidence first. He didn't send him through a year of leadership training (though there's nothing wrong with that). God simply answered every insecurity with one simple promise: *"I will be with you."* That was it. He didn't give him a pep talk. He didn't give him step-by-step plan. But what He gave him was His presence. And that presence was the very thing that allowed Moses to show up even while feeling completely unprepared.

And honestly? I can relate to that more than I ever expected to.

Your Story — The Calling You Didn't See Coming

If you've followed my ministry for a while, you may have heard this story...

I never intended to be a worship leader. Like...not on my radar. Not on my dream board. Not even in my prayers. What *was* on my radar? Becoming the next Amy Grant. (Side note: I still stand by my Amy Grant blazer. Iconic. Timeless. Let's not talk about it.)

But while I was imagining record deals, the Lord was whispering something completely different:

"You're going to be a worship leader."

And here's the wild part:

I didn't knock on a single door. Not one. But God started opening them.

He opened them so wide I couldn't ignore it.

At age 26, I became a worship leader at my church.

At 27, I was leading worship for 1,000 women in Oklahoma.

Within a year, I was leading for more than 3,000 women.

I still look back and shake my head, thinking:

"Lord... You really did that."

And you know what?

I did it afraid.

Not the kind of fear that stops you —

the kind that makes your knees knock while your faith pulls you forward.

I did it unsure.

I did it feeling unqualified.

I did it still learning.

Still growing.

Still figuring myself out.

Still asking God, "Are You sure You want *me*?"

But I showed up anyway.

Why?

Because I discovered the same thing Moses did:

> *If God is with me, I can show up to any assignment He gives me — even when I don't feel ready.*

It was never about my confidence.

It was never about my perfection.

It was never about my résumé or my skillset.

It was always — **always** — about Him.

His strength. His assignment. His ability. His presence.

And I couldn't imagine living any other way.

You know what I've learned from Moses' story, my own story, and the countless stories of people God has used?

God doesn't choose the most put together... He chooses the most surrendered.

- Moses argued.
- Gideon hid in a winepress.
- Jeremiah told God he was too young.
- Esther wasn't even invited into her own destiny — she was chosen for it.
- Peter was impulsive.
- Mary was overlooked.
- David wasn't even considered.
- Paul was an enemy of the Church before he became a pillar of it.

And yet God breathed on each one and said:

"Yes. You."

Not because they were ready.

63

Not because they were perfect.

Not because they felt capable.

But because they were willing to show up with what they had...
and trust Him with the rest.

The Myth of "Ready"

Let me give you a truth that will change your life:

Ready is not a feeling. Ready is a decision.

"Ready" is what God makes you *as you move* — not before.

Most people think breakthrough happens *before* you take the
step. But breakthrough actually happens **when your foot hits
the ground.**

The courage you think you should have first?

You get it while you're walking.

The clarity you want to have before you begin?

It comes after obedience — never before it.

The confidence you think other believers have?

Nope. They just learned how to move with shaky knees.

This world trains us to believe readiness is what qualifies us.
But Scripture teaches the exact opposite:

God doesn't call the equipped — He equips the called.

The Lie of "I'm Not Enough"

Let me tell you something personal:

The enemy has tried everything he can to try and stop me from
living out God's plans for my life. He's made many attempts to
whisper me into hesitation. To question. To Doubt. Not with
fear —but with the lie:

"You're not enough for this."

Not enough experience.

Not enough knowledge.
Not enough voice.
Not enough stability.
Not enough consistency.
Not enough strength.
Not enough background.
Not enough perfection.
The enemy always attacks identity before assignment.
He did it with Eve.
He did it with Jesus.
He does it with you.
Because if he can convince you that you're "less than," he knows you won't show up fully.
But hear me:
God is not looking for "enough."
He is looking for YES.
And your yes, even a trembling one, is stronger than every lie hell has ever thrown at you.

Why Your Willingness Matters More Than Your Confidence
When Moses finally stepped into obedience — even reluctantly — everything changed.
Why?
Because:
Moses didn't part the Red Sea. God did.
Moses didn't bring water from a rock. God did.
Moses didn't free Israel. God did.
Moses didn't carry the glory cloud. God did.

All Moses did was show up where God told him to go.

Your life will shift the moment you realize that what God calls you to is not about you, but about Him.

Your job is obedience.

God's job is outcome.

Your part is to show up.

His part is to breathe on it.

Your part is to take the next step.

His part is to light the path.

Your part is surrender.

His part is power.

You don't need to bring perfection —just yourself.

You don't need to bring answers —just willingness.

You don't need to bring confidence —just trust.

God can do more with a someone who shows up "not fully ready" than He can with a someone who has a Ph.D waiting for the perfect timing that never arrives. And if you choose that path —that simple, brave, obedient path of showing up —you will be amazed at what God can do through a willing heart.

So don't sit on the sidelines of your own calling.

Don't wait for confidence to catch up.

Don't wait for the "perfect moment" to appear.

If God is whispering... He is already equipping.

And if He is nudging... it's because He's already gone ahead of you.

Show up.

With shaky knees if you have to.

That's how extraordinary stories begin — with an ordinary person who finally stopped waiting to feel worthy and simply said yes.

Anchor Scriptures

"I will be with you." Exodus 3:12
   God's answer to insecurity is always Himself.

"Do not be afraid... for the Lord your God is with you wherever you go." Joshua 1:9
   Strength comes from His presence, not your personality.

"But the Lord said, 'Do not say, I am too young.'" Jeremiah 1:7
   God removes excuses before He releases purpose.

"My power works best in weakness." 2 Corinthians 12:9
   Your gaps are where His glory shines.

* * *

What I Learned — Chapter 6

How God Uses Ordinary, Imperfect, Still-Healing People to Do Extraordinary Things

   I learned that God has never once waited for me to feel "ready" before inviting me into something meaningful. He's not looking for perfect, put-together people — He's looking for willing ones. People who show up with shaky knees, tender hearts, and a simple, "Lord... I'm here."

* * *

THINK ABOUT IT

1. Where have I been waiting to feel "ready" before obeying God?
2. What step have I been avoiding because I don't feel qualified enough?
3. What would change if I trusted God with *outcome* instead of carrying the pressure myself?
4. Where have I seen God use my willingness more than my confidence?

Prayer

Lord, thank You that You don't wait for me to be perfect — You simply ask me to be willing. Teach me to trust Your presence more than my own readiness. Give me courage to step into the things You've called me to, even when I feel uncertain or afraid. Just as You were with Moses, be with me in every assignment, every invitation, every moment of obedience. Help me show up where You've placed me, knowing that You will supply everything I need as I move with You.

I surrender my insecurities, my doubts, and my timeline — and I choose to show up anyway. Amen.

7

The Rhythm of Heaven

Why Rest Is Not Optional for Your Purpose

* * *

I'm sure you've noticed by now that the world moves at a completely different speed than the way God does things. The world pushes fast, loud, frantic... and without even realizing it, we start trying to live the life God planted in us at that same speed. But here's the truth: we can't. It doesn't work. It won't last. And it definitely won't produce the kind of fruit our soul is craving.

Because here's what I've learned:

God doesn't form you in frenzy. He forms you in stillness.

The person you're becoming — the strong, steady, rooted woman (or man!) who walks in purpose and discernment — isn't shaped in hustle. Hustle may get things done... but it won't grow you in the long-run. It won't anchor you. And it won't prepare you for the weight of what God actually wants to put in your hands.

Stillness will.

Quiet will.

Those moments when you stop trying to carry the whole world on your shoulders and finally breathe again?

That's where God does His best work.

We don't like to admit it, but the world has trained us to think purpose is found in constant motion: *"Do more. Be more. Prove more. Don't ever slow down."*

But heaven doesn't sound anything like that. Heaven doesn't shout. Heaven whispers.

And that whisper sounds a lot like Psalm 46:10:

"Be still and know that I am God."

Now, I used to think being still meant doing nothing — like a spiritual time-out. But then I dug into the Hebrew, and it blew my mind. "Be still" actually means "let your hands drop... relax your grip... stop trying to force this... turn your attention back to Him."

It's not about inactivity.

It's about **alignment**.

It's a heart posture that gently says,

"Lord, You lead. I'll follow."

Stillness doesn't pull you away from your calling — it positions you *for* it. Isn't that good! It quiets the noise long enough for you to hear the One voice that matters.

And I'll tell you something else:

Stillness isn't the opposite of movement.

Stillness is what gives your movement meaning.

It's what gives you clarity when everything feels muddy.

It's what helps you tell the difference between a 'good' opportunity and a God assignment.

It's where anxiety loosens its grip because your soul finally gets to breathe again. It's the peaceful revelation you're learning that God never goes at the pace this world offers. He has His own perfect timing for everything!

It's where the Holy Spirit can actually get a word in edgewise. And if you're a woman reading this, you know that to be true! LOL!

The Meaning of Rest

In order to understand how important rest is in our life, Scripture is where that truth is revealed, because God didn't just suggest rest — He modeled it. In Genesis, after every act of creation, God stepped back, looked at what He made, and said, "It is good." And then He rested. Why? Because rest is part of the rhythm of heaven.

Work and wonder.

Movement and stillness.

Doing and beholding.

Let's think about this: If God wove rest into the very beginning of the world, then it's not supposed to be optional for us — it's essential. It's holy. It's where our heart recalibrates and our soul settles into who He says we are.

When we don't take time to rest it's almost as if we're saying, "Lord, I'd rather follow the example this world offers instead of the example You've given me." And then we wonder why we become short-fused, overwhelmed, exhausted, and not living out our true purpose.

In a recent deep dive, I came to a deep discovery in Hebrews 4 and I think it'll blow your mind. It calls this type of rest our "Sabbath-rest," and get this: that Greek word *sabbatismos* doesn't actually mean one day off a week. Say what!? It means a *continual rest* — a daily returning... a rhythm of trust you live from, not a little break you squeeze into your schedule.

Rest isn't a vacation.

It's a dwelling place.

It's not a nap.

It's a knowing.

It's not a break from life.

It's the place where life gets poured back into you.

And friend... this is the place where your identity stops wavering.

This is where your boundaries make sense again.

This is where calling becomes clear instead of confusing.

This is where the lies that used to scream at you suddenly lose their power.

This is where peace stops visiting you and starts living **in** you.

That's the rhythm of heaven.

It's never frantic.

It's never chaotic.

It's never pressured or hurried.

It's always steady. Sacred. Holy.

You weren't created for burnout. That's a symptom this world hands out like candy — but it has never been a symptom of God's leading. Burnout shows up when we're carrying things He never asked us to carry... running at speeds He never asked us to run... and trying to hold the universe together with our own two hands.

But Jesus?

He only ever offered one prescription for a heavy life - Matthew 11:28:

"Come to me, all of you who are weary and carry heavy burdens, and I will give you rest."

He didn't say,

"Work harder and I'll reward you."

"Fix everything and then come to Me."

"Run faster and maybe you'll earn a break."

No... He simply said:

Come.

Come when you're drained.

Come when you're overwhelmed.

Come when the pressure is too much.

Come when the weight you're carrying doesn't match the size of your shoulders.

Why?

Because rest isn't a luxury in the Kingdom — it's a lifeline.

The kind of rest Jesus talks is much deeper than we can imagine.

It's soul-rest.

Heart-rest.

Rest that reaches the places in you no amount of sleep can touch.

The Greek word for "rest"—**anapausis**—means:

- renewal
- refreshing
- intermission from toil
- the settling of the soul
- inward quiet even when life is loud

In other words, Jesus wasn't offering a break.

He was offering a **reset**.

You were created for abiding — for staying connected to the One who strengthens you from the inside out. Abiding is what keeps the roots of your life nourished even when everything around you feels dry. It's living grounded. Living at ease. Living present. Living held. Living unveiled.

God never intended rest to be a reward at the **end** of your strength.

He designed it to be the place you *start* from. Phew!

And here's the beauty of it:

When you rest in Him, you start to see the truth of who you are again. The noise settles. The accusations soften. The old fears lose their grip. And suddenly, you have hope again.

It's in that rested place where the person you used to be — the one who dreamed, trusted, believed, hoped — finally meets the person you're becoming. And in that meeting? Something in you clicks. Aligns. Heals. Strengthens.

For the first time in a long time...

you feel whole.

Not because life is perfect.

Not because everything is done.

Not because you've somehow become superhuman.

But because **you're resting in the arms of the One who will always, always carry what you can't. So rest. God's got you surrounded.**

* * *

What I Learned — Chapter 7

Why Rest Is Not Optional for Your Purpose

I learned that rest is not optional — it's holy. God wasn't asking me to hurry; He was inviting me to breathe. Stillness with Him became the place where clarity returned, peace settled, and the person I'm becoming finally had room to grow.

* * *

THINK ABOUT IT

1. Where in your life do you move at a pace God never asked you to keep?
2. When was the last time you felt truly rested — not just physically, but spiritually?
3. What lie have you believed about rest?
4. Read Hebrews 4:9 and Psalm 46:10. What stands out to you in this season?
5. If rest is the launchpad for purpose, what is one daily rhythm God is inviting you to begin?

PRAYER

Father, thank You for creating a rhythm of life that doesn't crush me, but restores me.

Teach me the beauty of stillness. Help me drop the hurry, release the pressure, and return to the pace You designed for me. Most importantly, show me how to come back to You —not just in crisis, but in rhythm. Help me build a life where rest isn't rare, but natural.

Lord, settle my soul. Quiet the noise. Align my heart to the rhythm of Heaven.

Restore the person I'm becoming and strengthen me to walk boldly into the life You planted in me. Amen.

8

The Pace of Purpose

Learning to Walk with God Without Rushing Your Own Life

* * *

We tend to think life is supposed to move like a pressure cooker — or like a Chic-fil-A fast food lane. But when you really pay attention to the way God works, life is actually a lot more like a crock pot. Slow. Intentional. Layered. Nothing rushed. Nothing wasted. Everything developing in its own time.

And one of the clearest pictures of this in Scripture is David. Not David the giant-slayer, or David the king, or even David the psalmist. I'm talking about David the teenager — the shepherd boy, the youngest son, the one his own father didn't even consider worth bringing inside when Samuel arrived to anoint the next king - just as we talked about in Chapter 2.

We love to talk about the moment Samuel poured oil on his head, because it feels big and dramatic. But we forget the part that reveals the heart of God: David was anointed in *one moment*, but he didn't become king for a good *fifteen years.* Fifteen years of ordinary days. Fifteen years of tending sheep, playing the harp, running from danger, hiding, living in caves, running for his life, learning how to trust God, and being shaped in ways no platform or spotlight could ever do.

While the world says, "Hurry up, you're falling behind," God was saying to David, "You're right on time." While culture pushes us to move faster and achieve more, God told David, "Stay in the field. I'm building something in you long before anyone sees it." His becoming didn't happen overnight. It was slow, holy formation — the kind that happens when you're simply living, listening, and walking with God.

David wasn't late.

He wasn't overlooked by God.

And he wasn't behind.

He was being developed. Quietly. Deeply. Purposefully.

God wasn't just preparing a king.

He was forming a heart that could *carry* a kingdom.

And that kind of becoming never happens in a pressure cooker. It happens at the pace of the Holy Spirit — steady, patient, and intentional. The same pace God invites you into today. Not rushed. Not frantic. Not fueled by fear or comparison, but shaped day by day as you walk with Him.

Purpose doesn't show up in leaps—it unfolds in layers. And when you finally step into it, it doesn't knock the wind out of you. It settles you. It matures you. It reveals itself slowly as you walk with the Lord... not as you chase life down like you're running after butterflies with a net.

Speaking of butterflies—let's go there for a second.

The Butterfly and the Pace of Becoming

There's this moment in a butterfly's life where everything looks still. Too still. So still you'd think nothing is happening. It's wrapped up in a cocoon—hidden, quiet, motionless.

But inside? Oh, everything is happening. Purpose is forming. Identity is being shaped. Wings are growing. Strength is building. Transformation is taking place in the dark, in the quiet, in the unseen.

And here's the reality:

If someone tries to rush that process—cuts open the cocoon to "help"—the butterfly doesn't make it. Why? Because the struggle inside the cocoon is what strengthens the wings. Just as David's journey to becoming King was. It's the slow formation, not the fast rescue, that prepares it to fly. That prepared David to become King.

Purpose works the same way.

There are seasons when you feel hidden—not forgotten, just protected while God works on something deep inside you. Seasons when you feel stuck—but He's strengthening things you can't see yet. Seasons when everyone else seems to be soaring and you're still wrapped up in a process that feels slow and uncomfortable.

But rushing it? Forcing it? Breaking open the cocoon before God says "now"?

That'll rob you of the strength you need for what's next.

Purpose doesn't need speed.

It needs surrender—to the pace God picked for your becoming.

The butterfly comes out right on time—not early, not late, but in the exact moment it's ready to fly. And so will you.

When Waiting Feels Like Wasting

Can I be real with you? Many times in my life I've felt that rush—the one this world keeps preaching. The pressure to move faster, do more, achieve big. And if I'm not careful, it creeps in and whispers, *"You're not doing enough. You're falling behind."*

But here's what I've learned—and honestly, I'm still learning it every day: when I try to rush what God meant to keep on simmer in that crock pot on low, it never ends well. It turns into an Ishmael.

I'll dig deeper into that revelation in my *Prothesis* book, but I can't skip past it here because it's too important.

Remember Abraham and Sarah? God gave them a promise, but waiting felt impossible. So they tried to "help" God out. And what happened? They created a plan that wasn't His plan.

I've been there. Maybe you have too—thinking, *"If I don't make something happen now, I'll miss my opportunity."* But every time I've tried to force God's timing, I've ended up frustrated, exhausted and anxious.

Here's the truth that's changed me: even though the years keep ticking by and I'm not getting any younger, there is **beautiful growth in the waiting**. And the bigger truth? Waiting doesn't mean God's purpose isn't happening. It actually is—every single day you wake up and live the life He gave you.

Reading scripture. Spending time with the Lord in prayer. Loving your family. Showing up at church. Those daily rhythms we sometimes call "ordinary" or even "monotonous"? They're not wasted. They're the foundation for the bigger dreams we're praying for.

Because how we choose to live out the small, daily commitments—that's what shapes the big picture. It all comes down to one word: **wait**.

So breathe. Just breathe in this season and wait. Don't sprint ahead of God. Let Him simmer what He's creating inside you. And when the timing is perfect—and it will be perfect—it'll come to pass.

But don't miss this: every single day is part of the plan. Every step matters. This is the pace of purpose.

Steps, Not Sprints

Just when you think the butterfly lesson couldn't get any clearer, Scripture steps in with a Psalm David wrote long after the caves and the battles and heartbreaks. This is older David - the weather, seasoned, been-there-done-that David. The David who has seen God show up slowly, faithfully, and consistently over a lifetime.

I like to imagine him sitting down, maybe with gray in his beard, a softness in his eyes and a knowing smile - speaking to a younger generation the very thing he had learned the long way:

> "The Lord directs the steps of the godly. He delights in every detail of their lives.....I have been young, and now am old." Psalm 37:23, 25

And that is why I love this verse for a thousand reasons is the depth he wrote it from, but mostly for one small, quiet word that we may not always catch, but it changes everything:
Steps.
Not leaps.
Not lightning bolts.
Not overnight moments.

Not somersaults.

Not speed.

Just... **steps.**

Purpose moves in steps — one little, ordinary, unimpressive step at a time. A conversation that felt small. A moment you almost brushed off. A gentle nudge in your spirit you tried to ignore. A "yes" you whispered while trembling. A decision nobody saw but Heaven celebrated.

Steps are slow.

Steps take trust.

Steps require patience — not rush.

And the part that gets me every single time?

God delights in every detail.

Every.

Single.

Detail.

The long seasons. The cocoon seasons. The detours. The pauses. The days you felt stuck. The days you wondered if you missed it. The days you whispered, "Lord... when?"

He delights in all of it because He sees more than the moment —

He sees the masterpiece being formed inside the moment.

You see delay; **He sees development.**

You see stillness; **He sees strengthening.**

You see confusion; **He sees construction.**

You see a cocoon; **He sees wings forming.**

Psalm 37:23 is God whispering:

"You don't need the whole map...

just take the next step I put in front of you."

You don't need the timeline. You don't need the platform. You don't need the spotlight. You don't need the speed. You need

His pace.

His guiding.

His direction.

His whisper saying, "This way... keep walking with Me."

You see, purpose is never built in your rush. It's built in His leading.

And the pace He sets?

It's not meant to frustrate you —it's meant to **protect** you.

Think about that:

He directs your steps.

And He delights in your details.

Who does that?

Only a Father who is not in a hurry.

Purpose never skips process.

Purpose grows through process.

And the person God is shaping you into?

You don't need speed to get there.

You need **presence.**

Awareness.

Stillness.

Trust.

And steps — small, steady, God-led steps.

You don't have to sprint toward your destiny.

You just have to walk with the One who already knows the way.

David lived long enough to see that God was never late — not once. And at the end of his life, with the wisdom of someone who had seen God weave purpose through every season, he left us with this reminder:

"I have been young, and now am old; yet I have never seen

the righteous forsaken..." Psalm 37:25

* * *

What I Learned — Chapter 8

Learning to Walk with God Without Rushing Your Own Life

I learned that God's purpose never moves at the speed this world pushes on us. It moves at His pace—slow enough to shape us, steady enough to strengthen us, and patient enough to grow us layer by layer. I learned that waiting isn't wasted at all; it's where wings are formed, roots go deep, and confidence is built quietly in the hidden seasons. And most of all, I learned that purpose unfolds in steps, not sprints—small, ordinary, faithful steps with a God who delights in every detail along the way.

* * *

THINK ABOUT IT

1. Where do you feel like you're "behind," and what could shift if you began trusting the pace God has set instead of the pace the world demands?
2. What part of your life right now feels like a cocoon — still, hidden, or slow — and how might God be strengthening you in that quiet place?
3. Take a moment to think about your journey so far. Were the biggest shifts really "sudden," or were they built on small steps you didn't realize mattered?

4. What would it look like to give yourself permission to walk instead of rush?
5. Read Psalm 37:23 again slowly. What word stands out to you today — directs, steps, or delights?

PRAYER

Lord, teach me how to walk at Your pace. Give me eyes to see purpose growing in slow places.

Give me strength for the days that feel still. Give me peace in the cocoon moments where transformation takes time. And give me courage to keep moving forward in the rhythm You've designed for my life. Thank You that You delight in every detail of my life. I choose to delight in Your pace. Amen.

9

Where Purpose Meets Real Life

Turning the Seed Into the Life God Planted

* * *

There comes a moment when everything God's been working on inside you... starts showing up on the outside. All the healing, boundaries, courage, discipline, rest, and pace He's been building in you finally begin to take shape in your real, actual life.

Because here's the thing:

Purpose doesn't just live in your heart. It lives in your hands. Your routines. Your choices. Your daily rhythms. Your everyday moments. Your thought life.

Purpose isn't something you wait for "someday." It's something you walk in today—in the life you already have.

But here's the part we forget and that we've been talking about throughout this book:

Purpose rarely begins with a big moment.

It usually begins with something small.

Sometimes insultingly small.

Let me show you what I mean.

The Dime That Turned Into Destiny

There's this story about a woman named Martha Berry back in the early 1900s. She had a God-dream burning inside her to start a school for kids who had no access to education. But here's what she didn't have: money, backing, credentials.

She just had a calling.

So she did something bold:

She asked for help.

She managed to get a meeting with Henry Ford—yes, *that* Henry Ford, the giant of industry. She shared her heart, her vision, her purpose.

And do you know what he did? He laughed. Then tossed her a dime.

Imagine that moment. The sting. The humiliation. Ten cents for a God-dream?

But Martha didn't crumble. She didn't walk away defeated—though I'm sure she felt it. She didn't bury her calling. She didn't decide she "must have heard God wrong." Instead, she took the dime and went to the store. Bought two packets of flower seeds. Planted them. Sold the flowers. Took the profit, bought more seeds, planted again. Over and over, quietly, faithfully—she multiplied that dime.

And eventually? She saved enough money to open the school God had placed inside her heart.

Years later, she went back to Henry Ford and told him what she'd built from the dime he tossed at her. He was so stunned he wrote her a check—not for pennies, but for millions.

But here's the part I want you to hear:

That school still exists today.

Yes—today. Over 120 years later.

What started with a dime is now Berry College in Georgia— still educating, still changing lives, still standing because one woman refused to despise the small.

That's purpose. That's obedience. That's faithfulness in motion.

The Scripture That Wraps Around This Story

This is where Galatians 6:9 comes alive in full color:

> "So let's not get tired of doing what is good.
>   At just the right time we will reap a harvest of blessing
>   if we don't give up." Galatians 6:9

Let's break this open for a second a little deeper, because this verse is not a "hang in there" verse. It's a blueprint for purpose.

"Doing what is good" — Greek: *kalopoieō*
It means:

- doing the God-thing
- the right thing
- the obedient thing
- the holy thing

88

- the purposeful thing
- the thing He nudged you to do even when it feels tiny

It's purposeful action in the direction of His calling.

"Don't get tired" — Greek: *egkakeō*
This means:

- don't lose heart
- don't give up internally
- don't talk yourself out of what God talked you into
- don't let disappointment rewrite your identity
- don't let slow progress convince you God isn't working

It's not about physical exhaustion —
it's about **protecting your spirit from discouragement.**

"At just the right time" — Greek: *kairos*

- This is not ordinary time (*chronos*).
- This is **God-appointed time.**
- The moment He has prepared, aligned, and breathed on.
- You can't rush kairos.
- You can't performance your way into it.
- You can't panic your way into it.
- Kairos arrives when obedience meets God's timing.

"We will reap a harvest" — Greek: *therizō*

- This isn't "maybe."
- This isn't "if you're lucky."

- This is a **promise**:
- If you sow what God tells you to sow,
- you *will* harvest what God intends you to harvest.

"If we don't give up" — Greek: *mē ekloumenoi*
  Literally:

- don't loosen your grip
- don't unravel
- don't quit before the breakthrough
- don't walk away from the field God told you to plant

The only way to miss the harvest is to stop sowing before God is finished growing.

What This Means for You

Scripture says, "Do not despise the day of small beginnings." And maybe you're thinking, "But Lord, I've been doing the small things for so many years I've lost count..." I get it. I really do. And I'm sure more of us are there than not. But stop and reflect for a second:

    What if the habits you've been wrestling with—the ones that feel so ordinary—are actually connected to the bigger things you've been praying for?

    When Martha Berry bought those seeds with her dime, she didn't just toss them in the dirt and walk away. She had to water them. Wait for them to grow. Prepare them to sell. Then go back to the store and buy more seeds. Over and over. Quietly. Faithfully. Disciplined. She had to keep doing the same thing over and over.

And it's the same way with us.

The big dreams we have? They're built on the small disciplines we'd rather skip.

Want to know what's crazy for me? I never realized how laundry was part of that lesson.

Now, you might be asking, *"What on earth does laundry have to do with God's purpose?"*

Well... let me tell you what the Lord showed me.

Laundry has always been my nemesis. I could keep a clean house—even while raising kids and juggling ministry—but laundry? That was my dread. And if I'm honest, it wasn't because I didn't have time. Sure, there were seasons where life was crazy, but most weeks? There were pockets of time I could've done it. The truth? I didn't want to.

I had no problem washing and drying. It was the putting away that I disliked. And that wasn't anyone's fault but mine.

But little by little, God started teaching me something through that pile of clothes: discipline matters. He nudged me to set aside time every week—not just to wash and dry, but to finish the job. To put it away.

And here's what blew my mind: that tiny discipline grew me more than I could've imagined. It wasn't about laundry—it was about learning to steward the small things. Because if I can't handle the things I don't want to do now, how will I handle the things I don't want to do when my big dreams come true?

Get it?

The pause you're in might be wrapped in tiny little discipline lessons God wants you to learn which is all a part of the bigger picture. And maybe the thing you've been ignoring—the laundry, the budgeting, the early mornings, the healthy habits—is the very thing God is using to shape you for what's next.

So don't despise the small beginnings. Don't roll your eyes at the ordinary. Don't think the unseen doesn't matter.

Because it does.

It's building something in you. Something strong. Something steady. Something that can carry the weight of the dream you've been praying for.

So here's the takeaway: purpose isn't waiting for someday— it's happening today. In the seeds you plant. In the habits you build. In the laundry you fold. In the prayers you whisper. In the choices nobody sees but Heaven celebrates.

Don't underestimate the ordinary. Don't despise the small beginnings. Every little act of faithfulness is shaping the person you're becoming and preparing you for the dream God placed inside you.

So keep showing up. Keep tending the seeds. Keep trusting the process. Because one day, you'll look back and realize the small things weren't small at all—they were the very steps that led you into the life God dreamed for you.

$$* * *$$

What I Learned — Chapter 9

Turning the Seed Into the Life God Planted

I learned that God can take the smallest seed — a tiny beginning, a simple act of faith — and grow it into something far beyond what I imagined. Purpose doesn't start fully formed; it starts with a seed and a decision to keep planting. And yes, God can teach you a beautiful life-changing lesson from laundry.

* * *

THINK ABOUT IT

1. What small "dime" has God placed in your hands right now?
2. Where have you grown tired of doing good because progress looks slow?
3. What would it look like to plant seeds again — even if the beginning feels unimpressive?
4. How might God be preparing a *kairos* moment you can't see yet?
5. What harvest might be tied to your faithfulness today?

PRAYER

Father, thank You for trusting me with small beginnings. Teach me how to plant what You've given me, to nurture what You've placed inside me, and to stay faithful when the results look slow. I surrender my "dime," my seeds, my little beginnings, and I ask You to breathe on them.

Bring Your *kairos* at the right time. And help me walk — faithfully, steadily — in the purpose You planted in me. Amen.

10

Unveiled Again

Go Live the Life God Planted in You

* * *

There comes a moment in every person's journey with God when the questions quiet down, the excuses lose their grip, and the fog finally begins to lift.

It's that moment when you realize:

"I can't just hear about purpose anymore. I can't just dream about it. I have to walk in it."

One small step at a time.

Everything you've walked through in this book—healing, boundaries, identity, rest, rhythm, courage, obedience—has been leading you right here:

to the moment you stop waiting for clarity

and start moving with God.

And if you're wondering,

"How will I know I'm ready?"

Here's the truth: you won't. Not fully. Not completely. Because purpose rarely comes wrapped in certainty.

Most of the time, it comes wrapped in a quiet nudge and a trembling yes.

And that's exactly where Deborah comes in.

The Deborah Moment

Deborah's story in **Judges 4 and 5** is one of the most powerful reminders that obedience and faith go hand in hand. Israel had been oppressed for 20 years under King Jabin. Fear was everywhere. No one wanted to lead. The men who should have stepped up? They froze.

But Deborah heard God's voice. She called Barak and said:

> *"This is what the Lord, the God of Israel, commands you: Call out 10,000 warriors... and I will call out Sisera... along with his chariots and warriors to the Kishon River. There I will give you victory over him!"* Judges 4:6–7

Did you catch that?

"I will give you victory."

Not *might*. Not *maybe*.

God declared the outcome before the battle even began.

And when Barak hesitated, Deborah didn't shrink back. She said:

> *"Very well, I will go with you. But you will receive no honor in this venture, for the Lord's victory over Sisera will be at the hands of a woman."* Judges 4:9

95

Then came the moment that changes everything:

> *"Then Deborah said to Barak, 'Get ready! This is the day the Lord will give you victory over Sisera, for the Lord is marching ahead of you.'"* Judges 4:14

That's the key:

"The Lord is marching ahead of you."

Victory wasn't something they had to fight for—it was something they fought from.

Deborah understood this truth:

When God calls you, He goes before you.

When He sends you, He fights for you.

When He speaks, His word is already settled.

That's faith. That's confidence. That's living unveiled—stepping out even when fear whispers, *"You're not ready."*

Deborah didn't wait for everything to be perfect. She didn't wait to feel qualified. She didn't wait for applause. She simply said yes. And that yes changed history.

What This Means for You

Living unveiled again means walking out what God has called you to do—even when it feels scary, even when you don't have all the answers. It means trusting that the same God who spoke to Deborah is speaking to you. And if He goes before you, you don't have to be afraid.

Faith isn't the absence of fear—it's moving forward anyway because you know Who walks with you.

Your Time to Step Forward

Everything God planted in you has been growing beneath the surface—the calling, the courage, the clarity, the strength, the voice, the heart, the purpose.

This isn't about becoming someone different. It's about becoming who you've always been. Not the "ready" version. The obedient version. The willing version. The surrendered, *"God, I'm here"* version. And if you need a picture of what that looks like, let me tell you about Jackie Pullinger.

At 22 years old, Jackie boarded a ship with nothing but a one-way ticket and a whisper from God: *"Go."* No big plan. No guaranteed support. Just faith.

She landed in Hong Kong and walked straight into the Kowloon Walled City—a place most people avoided. It was a maze of crumbling buildings, ruled by triads, thick with drugs, crime, and hopelessness. It was the kind of place where light seemed swallowed by darkness.

Jackie didn't arrive with a platform or a strategy. She arrived with faith. She started small—teaching music, loving kids, praying simple prayers. Then she opened a youth center. Later, she founded **St. Stephen's Society**, a ministry that would help thousands of addicts find freedom and new life in Jesus.

Her work wasn't glamorous. It was gritty. It was slow. It was dangerous. But Jackie kept saying yes—yes to God's whisper, yes to the hard places, yes to the people everyone else overlooked.

Decades later, her impact is undeniable. Entire lives transformed. Families restored. Addicts set free. Even the Hong Kong government recognized her work because it changed the city from the inside out.

Here's the revelation:

Jackie didn't wait for perfect conditions. She didn't wait to feel qualified. She didn't wait for applause. She simply said yes. And that yes changed everything.

Faith = Purpose = Action.

Faith isn't just believing God can—it's stepping out like He already has.

That's what living unveiled again looks like. It's not loud. It's not flashy. It's not about having all the answers. It's about trusting the One who goes before you and taking the next step— even if your knees are shaking.

Because here's the promise:

"Your own ears will hear Him. Right behind you a voice will say, 'This is the way you should go...'" Isaiah 30:21

And when He whispers, *"Go,"* you can move with confidence because **"the Lord is marching ahead of you."** Judges 4:14

So go.

Not in hurry.

Not in pressure.

Not in fear.

Go in obedience.

Go in identity.

Go in confidence.

Go in partnership with the God who chose you on purpose, for purpose.

And as you go, heaven goes with you.

This is your moment. Your assignment. Your yes.

Walk it out with courage and joy because He is with you.

Walk it out with the steady assurance that the One who planted these dreams inside you is the One who will bring them to life.

Go live the life God planted in you—and don't you dare look back.

* * *

What I Learned — Chapter 10

Go Live the Life God Planted In You

I learned that calling isn't a someday thing — it's a right-now thing. Everything God has been shaping, healing, pruning, strengthening, and awakening in me was leading to this: to walk unveiled again, to live on purpose, and to stop waiting for a permission slip that heaven already signed.

* * *

THINK ABOUT IT

1. What step have you been waiting to feel "ready" for — and is God simply asking you to obey instead?
2. Where have you been underestimating your calling because it doesn't look "big enough" yet?
3. What is one area of your life where God is whispering, "This is the way — walk in it"?
4. Have you buried any dreams God wants to resurrect?
5. What would faithfulness look like *today*, not someday?

PRAYER

Jesus, I don't want to just dream about purpose anymore —I want to walk in it. Show me the places You are leading me. Give me the courage of Deborah, the steady obedience of bamboo roots, and the confidence to follow Your voice even when the next step feels small. Grow what You've planted in me. Strengthen what You've rooted in me. And lead me into the life You designed long before I ever knew to ask for it. I say yes. Amen.

11

Conclusion

If you've made it to the end of this book, let me just say this straight up:

I'm proud of you.

Because somewhere between Chapter 1 and right now, you made a choice — maybe a whisper of a choice, maybe a trembling one — to become *unveiled* again. To peel back the layers you've been hiding behind. To breathe deeper than you have in a long time. To look your own story in the face and say, "Okay, God... let's keep going."

And that matters.

More than you know.

You didn't just read words on a page.

You let God stir something.

You let Him nudge, whisper, prod, and shine light in places you thought were too buried or too broken or too ordinary to matter.

But here's the truth — the truth I want you to walk away with burning bright in your spirit:

Nothing God plants stays small.

Nothing God breathes on stays hidden.
Nothing God begins ends in defeat.

You are stepping into a new season — not because everything around you suddenly changed, but because *you* did.

Some layers fell off.

Some lies got exposed.

Some courage woke back up.

Some identity clicked into place.

Some dreams got pulled out of storage and dusted off.

Some purpose started stretching its wings again.

And now?

Now it's time to live it.

To really live the life God planted inside you before you ever took your first breath.

Because you, my friend, are a walking testimony of "still becoming."

You're living proof that God can use the broken pieces, the healed pieces, the still-healing pieces, and the "I'm not sure yet how this fits" pieces — and turn it all into something that shines His glory.

You're not behind.

You're not late.

You're not disqualified.

You're not starting over.

You are **unveiled again** — and that is a miracle all by itself.

What Happens Now?

Now you get to walk it out.

This book wasn't the finish line.

It was the unlocking.

It was the clearing of the soil.

The uncovering of what got buried.

The gentle reminder that you're still in there.

The invitation to rise again.

And as you rise, as you walk, as you take the next obedient step... God will meet you in ways you couldn't have imagined ten chapters ago.

And This Is Only the Beginning

If this book awakened something in you — even a spark — stay close, because the journey continues.

My upcoming book **Prothesis: God's Purpose · My Pursuit** (releasing in 2026) is where we take this even deeper.

There, we walk into:

purpose

calling

alignment

obedience

and the daily rhythms that carry it all.

And because purpose isn't just something you learn — it's something you *live* — the **Holy Habits workbook** will walk right alongside you, giving you simple, steady rhythms that build a life aligned with Him.

This is all part of the same heartbeat of Unveiled Living — helping people experience the freedom Jesus already paid for, the identity He already gave them, and the purpose He already planted inside.

My Final Words to You

Go live.

Go dream again.

Go listen for His whisper.

Go take the next step.

Go walk in what He already sees in you.

Go let your life shine, not from overdoing it, but from abiding.

And when your feet hit the floor tomorrow, I pray the enemy sighs and says,

"Oh no...

they're awake again."

Because awakened, unveiled, surrendered people?

They change the world.

And now — you're one of them.

Afterword

A Note From Tracee:

Unveiled Living was birthed from a deep desire in my heart to help people live the way God intended — unveiled.

So many of us carry pieces of our past like a veil...

old shame, old battles, old labels, old lies...

things that made us feel disqualified or hidden.

But that is *not* the story Jesus has written for us.

2 Corinthians 3:16–18 says that **when we turn to the Lord, the veil is taken away**, and where His Spirit is — there is freedom. That's the heartbeat of Unveiled Living. Freedom. Clarity. Boldness. Real life with God, without the weight of the old covering what He's doing now.

I started this ministry because I wanted people to know they could live that way — not pressed down by what happened to them, but lifted by what Jesus already finished for them.

And now, the next step in that journey is **Prothesis** — coming in 2026.

If Unveiled Living is the invitation to walk unveiled, **Prothesis** is the daily blueprint for how to keep living that freedom out loud. It's the holy habits, the steady rhythms, the structure that strengthens your life to carry what God has entrusted to you.

If you want to stay connected or walk this journey with me, you can always find me at:

unveiledliving.org

I'm cheering you on as you keep stepping into the life God planted in you — unveiled, steady, and full of His freedom.

Living life unveiled,

Tracee

www.ingramcontent.com/pod-product-compliance
Lightning Source LLC
LaVergne TN
LVHW051417080426
835508LV00022B/3136